THAMES PATH POEMS

By David May

Illustrations Wendy Couchman

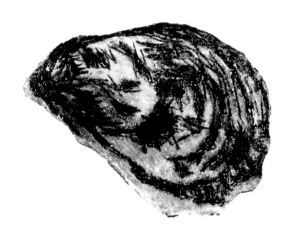

CONTENTS

Preface

Preface

Both of us have lived and worked in London and have family connections there going back many generations. In the summer of 2017 we decided to start walking the Thames Path in stages, along the lower tidal reach of the river from Erith in the east and up to Teddington Lock.

This collection of poems and illustrations looks at the engineered landscape of the banks of the Thames, buildings that shaped the vision of the capital city: disused sewage works; new pumping stations and incinerators; overgrown post-war bombsites; disused cranes, jetties and gantries; old lighthouses; new modernist concrete housing estates, factories, bridges, tunnels; historic Woolwich Arsenal currently being converted into sleek new Docklands apartments and the sculptured, shell-like structure, the Thames Barrier installation.

The order of the poems follows the four headings of the guidebook, *Walking the Thames Path* (Cicerone Press 2016):

- Erith to the Thames Barrier (8 m)
- Thames Barrier to Tower Bridge via Greenwich (9m)
- Tower Bridge to Putney via Vauxhall (10m)
- Putney to Teddington Lock via Eel Pie Island (13m)

David May
Wendy Couchman
Winchester 2021

Beginning Poem

William Wordsworth wrote of smog and
empire
Shops, towers and poetic theatrical domes
That opened up to the sky
But that was then and now is nigh
Two hundred years or more have flowed
past.

TS Eliot, a century ago, spoke of wasteland
The burial, and the desired dead
The unreality beneath the brown fog
And the crowded bridge of demobbed
uniformity
After the Great War.

But the soft, sweet Thames of sleek
modernity
Has meant the departure of the water
nymphs
To try to capture the essence of essential
life
Of what the capital was really like
One hundred years ago.

Half-century aged since I was young and
daft
I first walked along the old towpath

With Richard Mabey in an unofficial
countryside
Labouring away amongst the post-war
London Blitz
Beaten generation, the beginnings of
passionate rich.

And to today, the present time, to be in a
global pandemic
Robert Macfarlane's hotch-potch terrain
vague 'somewhat ugly but bizarre'
The walker's view that I now gaze upon
Jettery, jumbled yard and a sluggish canal.

A wilderness, a wild place to dream
unseen
Experience the magnetic magnitude of
Metropolis
Where migrant men and women work to
the bone
Refugees from a cruel domain in a foreign
dearth
Lightyears away, swimming in a hellish
river of earth.

Erith

We walked out of Erith electric railway
station
After travelling overground from Waterloo
East
The morning sun was blinding our eyes
We turned away to face due west
Towards the city which never rests
Where my coastal ancestors had barged
Moored in the rippled mudflats, at low
tide
Ready to embark on the high-rise trade
Across the German Sea.

The abandoned waterfront looked serene
A guerrilla war, location for Apocalypse
Now Heart of Darkness, the killing fields
Colonel Kurtz was waiting to be killed
We had to follow upriver to a jungle
hiding place
Where evil lurked in every shadow cast
Kentish marshland to Barking Reach
It was early May, after the cruellest month
And we were seeking Great Expectations.

Joseph Conrad wrote of a 'casual stroll'
along the words
Along the broad reach bankside in a
different era
To discover the unknown secrets of the
Empire

He illuminated the invisible moonlit
fantasy game
That led to the undisclosed secret transit
shed
Of a dreamscape to explore your heart and
mindset
A landscape to be discovered by chance,
by a feral dream
At the deep aquifer from whence the
London river came
Until the Dryad wrecked the peace and
tranquil stream.

A rotted baulk, an empty hulk that once
held prisoners
Before deportation to a seized aborigine
colony
On the other side of the red terrestrial
globe
An escaped convict seemed to be lurking
in the scrub
About to pounce on two poor, passing
travellers
I stared at the muddy rivulets slipping the
clay
Rabid reflections, refracted sunlight, a
prism of urban decay
No Thames barge, no sooty cutter from
Hartlepool
A terrible, threatening place to tempt the
soul.

Crossness

The Great Stink in 1858 caused your
immaculate creation
By Bazalgette, the civil engineer: the sewer
King Rat
Who built in Romanesque style: a sacred
cathedral of sludge
And red blood-stained, charcoal-furnaced
bricked earth
A glorious pumping station, shaped like a
cruciform
A cross of mirrored glass and man-made
machines
Facing east-west like a medieval chapel of
rest
In the same direction as the Norman
Conquest
Empire of the Sun found its Paradise Lost!

London migrant workers slaved to break
free
Carved out fatberg glaciers that flowed
from up Battersea
Liquids, solids and foul clay-ware drains
flowing
Into the sanguine East End settling pond of
cloudy blight
Blackened by the light, dragon insect's
delight
Basking floaters, boatmen, miniature
molluscs

Feeders of detritus, not quite clean enough
to consume
Now an oral memory, a perfumed garden
parade
No longer plying your personal scented,
dirty trade.

On the opposite bank I imagined my mad
London crowd
Ford Dagenham, Beckton and Becontree
Estate
Doreen married a demobbed airman from
the South-West
Her two siblings were foremen at the car
factory
Assembling motor vehicles for sale, stored
in a compound
In the landscape where wild birds once
nested
Ferry across to Rainham, sent to Essex –
thank God!
Let sleeping corpses lie, I say, they cannot
say hello mate
For they are lost in space, cremated in a
fully conscious state.

Sky-blue Barking Barrier sluice, raised in
royal salute
A floodgate of watery tears emerged from
the Northern Outfall
Where a young apprentice came of age,
one day
Witnessed a superintendent drink from a
sanitised chalice

To prove that the Engineer had turned the
water into wine
But my cup runneth over and spilled in my
psyche
I was waiting for him to keel over in a
mystic stupor
Dead as a doormat, poisoned on the
muddy threshold floor
To dream of filthy streams like James
Joyce.

As Wendy and I continued on our
Thameside walk
The sky above became bluer and the
clouds cleared our path
I heard birdsong, then I watched as she
earnestly trudged ahead
Towards where she was born, the magic
birthing pool
Royal Hammersmith Hospital, raised in
the Surrey hills
Cross Ness and Tripcock lighthouses
called out for us
To be safe with only a crumbling skeleton
crew
Then I thought I felt her lasting breath on
my sallow skin
In the warm breeze, blowing in from the
Orient.

The Thames Barrier Disaster

We had hoped that the 1928 Thames Flood
Disaster
Would not return to haunt any survival
doubts
Reading about the Princess Alice collision
in 1878
When six-hundred and fifty day-trip
passengers perished
Off Tripcock Point, near this modern
construction site
Drowned or poisoned by the Crossness
sewer fumes.

Watching ten curved-backed gates
submerge below
Like Black Sea serpents, escaping the
whaling ship
A shiny aluminium boathouse from
Narnia stands erect
Guarding us from the ice-maiden, the cruel
Snow Queen
Who thawed out the frozen St Lawrence
river estuary
And brought a terror, a titanic tsunami
flooding our space.

Yellow A-framed beams, raised ready for
another perfect storm
To quell the raging currents, arising from
Hurricane Montserrat
A ragged peak-tide of rough, rushing
London cataracts

We stood literally welded to the amazing
metallic sheen
Reflecting on the rampage, a Sahara
Desert-like apparition
Our real and present danger to life as we
know it, Jim?

Then the magic monster dived and
disappeared from the scene
And we were saved! The highest Spring
tide and gale had gone
The gateway had dropped into recessed
concrete cills
Barracked on the muddy silt-dredged
riverbed
For a moment the silenced canaries sang
again
All the way from Woolwich Arsenal to
Teddington.

We had all laid low, waited in fear until
the crisis passed
But there was always hope and pray we
would not capsize
But stay afloat and continue on our
journey upstream
Walking along the dry Thames Path, a
slow hike
From Erith Marsh to the furthest tidal
reach
Between the shores of Middlesex and
Surrey diocese.

Born in Barking (The Ferry)

I rode right across the wide river, my first
trip abroad!
From north to south, on board the free
Woolwich Ferry
Uncle Terry, my hero, was steering an
exciting new course
He soon soared away in the Merchant
Navy
And sailed the seven seas on Hadriania - a
sea shell company!

The National Union of Seamen looked
after Terrence John
Born in Ilford, hazel eyes and a claret-and-
blue tattoo
Signed on initially at London Victoria
Docks in April '58
South East Africa and Southampton on the
Castle line
Very good conduct on his service record –
but not all the time!

Sister Jude wrote that she'd been re-united
With our long-lost seafarer, discharged
after his last voyage
From deck boy to able-seamen
quartermaster
When offered a transfer to the royal Senior
Service

He had refused to accept the Queen's
shilling.

Today he lives down under in Western
Australia
Perth was his final dry dock, a favourite
port of call
Perchance to live the dream, leaving East
End reality
But every day he leaves the family home in
the hills
To make a pilgrimage to touch the hulls.

I stayed put on a different path, a
confirmed landlubber
Lacking any dark blue uniform or sea leg
trapeze
But that summer, when Wendy and I
walked ashore
I watched your ferryman turn broadside
Alongside where you showed us the
ropewalk.

Your poor parents did not want their
youngest son to go
And never see him again, lost amongst the
swirling waves
Devoured by Moby Dick and German
submarines
His two older brothers both worked beside
the grey
The irony, that you were the sweetness,
and the strong

Working the MV Sugar Carrier, importer
to Silvertown.

On our walk past the desolate row of
wharves and jetties
From Erith to Eel Pie Island in the sunset
west
I often thought of you Tel, refusing to be
submerged
Like your ancient mariner-ancestors from
Essex
Sailing cargo schooners out from the
Blackwater Estuary.

*(Dedicated to Uncle Terry Pickett, born in
Barking)*

Thamesmead

Barking Reach extends as far as
Thamesmead
And Bellmarsh Prison: England's
Guantanamo Bay
Film location for Kubrick's Clockwork
Orange
A dystopian horror story from the
modernist Sixties
'We've been concrete-framed' they all cried
out
A Peabody housing scheme your saving
grace.

Wendy and I encountered a bankside border control
Building a wall of silence and intimidation scene
As they turned around, avoiding any eye-contact
Two retired foot soldiers wounded in the line of duty
Not huddled in a gangland of smoking terrorism
Dressed to kill in Adidas, Under Armour and Nike.

We needed a South London passport for our protection
Money paid to Mad Frankie Frazer if he had lived
And the Richardsons, not the Kray Twins over here
Because they came from Bethnal Green in the East End
Blind Beggar, where Ronnie shot Jack the Hat
And Reggie knifed a rival at a nightclub.

A shrug of the padded tracksuit shoulder pads greeted us
'We come unarmed, not packing a punch' we whispered

'Only a bottle of water and a packed
lunch!'
Old folks' home from home, we quickly
turned inland
Heading for HMP, or Southwark Crown
Court
Gallions Point beckoned, our refuge place.

We stayed well out of sight, kept our heads
down
But not as far as Eltham, Well Hall and
Shooters Hill
Where Stephen Lawrence was sadly killed
on the streets
Of the South Circular ring road, near
Brownhill
A case of juvenile murder and double
jeopardy
Reversed by Act of Parliament and the
House of Lords.

A Slice of Reality

Left high and dry above the rising tide
On the Greenwich Mean Time
Overlooking the barking Isle of Dogs
Canary Wharf; No1 Canada Square
The dream of Margaret Thatcher
And a Canadian entrepreneur called Paul.

Richard Wilson has built half a ship
Floating on the River Thames
A Slice of Reality, whatever that means?
The artist invited us to go aboard
To walk the gangplank to oblivion
Admiral Lord Nelson's Victory cabin.

Royal Academician was sat in his art
gallery
Holding court, talking at his crew of
sycophants
Sat on a sculptured tripod throne
We joined the worshipping throng
Bought a Folkestone picture: '18 Holes'
Now we were art collectors, like Saatchi.

Sliced, ocean going sea-sand dredger
Bridge, poop and engine room
Exposed to the elements: wind and rain
Tea and a slice of cake, served on bone
china
A London trader still working on the
waves
We'll remember the genius of eccentricity.

The Limehouse Link

Fanny Kemble sang and danced on your
subterranean stage
Bright footlights lit the underworld Road
to Hades
Monty Python's Palin: 'now for something
completely different!'
'Sheer engineering chutzpah'- your boring
tunnel shield
The Eighth Wonder of the Wapping world
Dreamt up in the Mayflower pub in
Rotherhithe.

I glimpsed your magic steam-driven pump
house there
And Marc and his Pompey boy, Isambard
Kingdom Brunel
Prayed to the Assyrian Queen Semiramis
of Van
To spare the flood of the London
Euphrates river man
Created by Cornish mining engineers, like
Vazie
And Trevithick, the Camborne inventors of
steam.

They overcame Teredo Navalis, the
tunnelling shipworm
That crawl'd down the spiral staircase,
inside the caisson

Into the darkness of the burial chamber,
where men had died
Drowned, engulfed somewhere south of
Limehouse wharf
Below the proscenium arches of architect,
Inigo Jones
I thought I glimpsed the ghostly remains of
drillers' bones.

The miners sacrificed their own lives for
this ingenious conceit
Old Father Thames, the water serpent
hidden in the deep
Watched as I crossed over to the other side
of town
On the East London underground line
through to Surrey Docks
Our secret hideaway, a place to dream of
Babylon
The Limehouse Link to a utopian dream.

Rotherhithe

Through Limehouse Reach, past
Greenland Dock
We curved north around the edge of
Lower Pool
A tunnel emerged from the opium dens of
Chinatown
Where addicts and pedestrians crossed
over to the other side
Along the Thames pathway to oblivion.

Once smallpox ships raised anchor here or
thereabouts
Stinking decks were scrubbed with
sulphuric acid foam
Poorly patients were taken away from the
gangrene ghettoes
To the welcome stench of sewage farms
and power stations
Isolation chimneys incinerating dampened
patchwork dolls.

Into Bermondsey, south of the elevated
Tower Bridge
Shad Thames, a narrow street of iron
walkways crossing
Cherry Garden where Turner painted, *The
Fighting Temeraire*
As it berthed, dreading the final breaker's
yard
Wendy and I walked hand-in-hand to the
gantry platform
Looking across the river to Judge Jeffreys'
Execution Dock.

We lodged in a converted soot-stained
warehouse cell
But stayed awake all night, disturbed in
our sleep by goblins
And ghosts of Captain Cook returning
from the South Seas

The Pilgrim Fathers leaving to pray for
Protestant Puritans
Seeking a pure reformed church in New
England.

We heard the nightmare, homesick refrains
of drunken men
Who had drowned their souls in 'the
Greatest Bore'
The Brunels' tunnel of love, bubbling
beneath our bunks
Only to be awakened at dawn by the siren
horn
Of the Sea Princess, leaving on the
morning tide.

After breakfast, we walked on past Jacob's
Island
Once a stagnant slum, a grisly murder
scene from a tale
Where cruel Bill Sykes clubbed Nancy to
death in Oliver Twist
Charles Dickens' episodic tale of inner
London life
No port outwards, starboard home for
those slum-dwellers.

St Saviour's Dock was made by diverting
the River Neckinger
Where 'neckcloth' nooses were placed
around pirates' necks

Serenaded by the oriental aroma of
Chinese cassia
Drifting over from Jasmine and Cinnamon
Wharves
Le Pont de la Tour beckoned us, a table for
two rich travellers.

Onto the Angel and my Sixties playground
for the young
I drank porter ale from a Thames
brewhouse close by
Samuel Pepys was writing something with
quill and gall ink
James Abbott McNeil Whistler flew out
from a gilded cage
So I left my old memories, and piped
dreams far behind.

Wapping Stairs

Broken clay pipes, eroded pots, empty
oyster shells
Discarded by a passing river trade
Leaving the Pool of London
Going east towards the Estuary
On the twice daily rising tidal stream
Out to Tilbury and the German Sea.

The Marchioness Disaster cost fifty-one
lives
Struck Cannon Street Railway Bridge in
1989
On its way out to the glistening Thames
Barrier
Whilst Dancing Queen played on the
dance floor
Life and death caused by the dredger
Bowbelle
Whose captain was drunk on duty, gone to
hell.

The cruel coroner cut off the hands of the
faceless
For the identification parade, on the
mortuary slab
Those faceless bodies recovered by the
River Police
Brought back to Wapping Stairs and
Rotherhithe
Town of Ramsgate, Captain Kidd and the
Prospect
All closed their doors, out of respect for the
dead.

The Shard

I knew your engineer, my original role
model from abroad
In 172 Great Portland Street, I sat on the
next drawing board
The Somerset Levels mystic, sketched
models in 3-D
Before I left to find my own good fortune
teller.

One day King Kong will scale the faceted
facade
To sit under the twin spired jaws, a symbol
frozen in time
An empire state, a stainless-steel caricature
Opposite the classic masonry dome of St
Paul's.

Not a single shard? Prick up your ears, Joe
Orton!
A rival to the Burj Khalifa on the
waterfront of Dubai
The Petronas Twin Towers in Kuala
Lumpur
Does One World Trade Centre trump
9/11?

A post-modern pastiche of urban dream
machines and men
A phallic Tiffany Lamp lit by the New
York Sun

Catalogued in Petticoat Lane, Whitechapel
in the East End
Shard is a banned word for poets, like the
shimmer effect!

An angry upturned glass crocodile snout,
an alien insect trap
A hellish monster, reflecting an aura of its
own worse predator
A giant topsy-turvy dowel, a screw-bit
drill, a thrusting dagger
Through the heart of Southbank, forced by
the devil incarnate.

Lance the boil of Mammon, rancid barb-
infested spear of Midas
A javelin dipped in a maggoty rotted
corpse of pus-filled putrid Pan
Mounts a monumental stalagmite of
poisoned Satyr
And a grizzled shark's fin projecting from
a lairy orifice
Beneath the scaly scabs wiped under the
devil's forked tail

Wendy and I walked away from your
gleaming, blingy presence
Watching Winchester Shrews tout for their
own dirty trade
Before we imagined them going deep
underground
In Southwark's old diocese, south of the
River Thames.

Westminster Bridge Eulogy

I came upon the second crossing,
according to Belloc
Where Wordsworth stood and admired the
surrounds
Composed a sonnet, hid in an octagonal
cubby-hole:
'Ships, towers, domes, theatres and temples lie
Open unto the fields, and the sky'
Born of pure white stone from Portland
Bill.

Whistler, Turner and Monet painted,
Evelyn wrote:
'Hellish and dismal Clouds of SEA-COLE'
Passing under the Thames Path, before
County Hall
Old Westminster Bridge was forever
cursed thus
By the Archbishop's Lambeth Palace
ferrymen
For taking away their sacred Christian
livelihood.

Henry Fielding called out the 'Bridge of
Fools'
I dreamt of a true love next to me, not too
far away

Waterloo station terminus of the Southern
Railway
Where we began our cosmic trip to
rainbow's end
A new bridge has taken shape on the river
bend
In dead men's shoes of hard Cornish
granite stone.

Venetian larch piles driven deep into dark
blue clay
Encased in concrete, clad in ribbed rusty
steel
A Metropolitan Water Board crusty coat of
gold
Emblazoned with the Molesworth Arms,
Wadebridge
A member of the industrial revolutionary
guard
Opened up on a Queen's birthday, but she
did not attend.

Parliamentary green, Charles Barry's
gothic revival
Big Ben struck eight, to muffle moaning
corpses
Beneath seven elliptical spans of Greek
geometry

Where six people sadly died on 22 March
2017
Mad Khalid Masood killed innocent
passers by
A brave policeman stabbed to death on
sentry duty.

He protected our democratic right to
survive intact
PC Keith Palmer may you rest in peace on
our walk
Of shame, that no-one was beside you
when you died
But when we pass this way again, in our
pounded beat
This will be your London killing field:
'And all that mighty heart is lying still.'

(After William Wordsworth c.1802)

The Thames Path Walk

This is about walking beside the river
Heart of Darkness made me quiver
Expectations great, but may not deliver.

Towpath, where we headed due west
Hammersmith, from whence you came
Arsenal FC born in Woolwich Arsenal
Mortlake where the Boat Race ends
East End bovver boys in Bethnal Green
Silvertown built by Caribbean sugar
slaves.

Pimlico was a passport for Henry Tate
A bigger splash, beyond the sluice gate
Teddington Lock, the tidal lower reach
Hampton Court Maze where you got lost.

Winchester, where we began our poetic
trip
A cathedral city still bringing me down
London Bridge is not falling down!
Kingston-upon-Thames not fade away...

(After Robert Macfarlane)

Vauxhall

We spent the night at Vauxhall Pleasure
Gardens
A red-lit district back in its night-time,
pleasure seekers' day
When the uncivil engineer Bazalgette built
his culvert
The Embankment on reclaimed gravel
islands and marsh
Where Bronze Age bridge builders first
crossed the Thames
Protruding oak piers point towards the
first of many
Long before King John's knight templar
erected Fox Hall
Wendy had booked ahead to reserve our
seedy hostelry
At St George's Wharf, now the ugliest
building in town.

As we sat out on the balcony in the
evening air
Overlooking no. 49 Cheyne Walk, and my
old memories
My mind wandered to Mick Jagger and his
Faithfull girlfriend
Both sides now, where London drug busts
were framed

Hosting pyrotechnics, puppet shows and
music pageants
Right down to the riverbanks of indecency
and frown
Where we had walked that very morn
Hampshire poet Edward Thomas' hidden
gods and goddesses
That live beneath the roads. Well, I
thought of these sprites.

And the lost river of Effry still flowing
under the Thames Path
Took me back to the summer of '69, when I
slept out in Tivoli
Under a shady tree, close to a sculptured
Danish girl
Inspired Vokzal. 'What a merry day it is!'
sang Fanny
Boscawen, a Cornish maiden's name from
Arthur's myth
Genius loci: Handel composed trickling
water music in space
Where it is played every other day,
somewhere near here
We listened, but there was no sound, only
trafficking
It was time, time to spy on Nine Elms and
Battersea.

On the Central Line

You were born on the riverbank
During the Second World War
After the London Blitz
That bombed Putney Bridge Road.

You grew up near a vacant bombsite
On the Thames, near Wandsworth
Where you later returned to teach
And paint on Wapping High Street.

You lived there all alone in Towerside
Before heading back at the weekend
To a Hampshire country town
But in your heart, always a West End girl.

The mystic, magnetic pull led you back
Time and time again. You phoned:
London Calling! - my godsend
Travelling on the Central Line.

Hammersmith Bridge

Glorious livery in Kensington Harrods'
green and gold
Suspended, slung lowly across the River
Thames
Cast iron bridged, adorned with an
ornamental crown

William Tierney Clarke created an original
brand
Purpose-built for the Metropolitan Water
Board.

Like all great genii, it was doomed, fatally
flawed
Weak, narrow, under-designed from its
birthplace
Concealed broken anchorages were
earthed in hell
Hidden from the gods and goddesses that
lurk
With nymphs, slimy eels and silvery
serpents.

Joseph Bazalgette, the London sewer rat
Came afar to claim your Georgian heritage
To destroy the origin design, to inherit
your legacy
White-washed the brick facade in Portland
Stone
Before drowning your memory
downstream.

I stood and watched, from the northern
Hammersmith shore
As the Boat Race crews slid barely
underneath your deck
Oxford dark and Cambridge light blue
couture
A clash of colours, a mobile kaleidoscope
of elegance

The sleek wooden craft saluted, with eight
dipped blades.

Cutting through the murky surface, a
rainbow sheen
No bigger splash or catching crabs, that
would be obscene
But throughout the rival sporting scene,
you stood serene
Aloof, impervious to the baying crowds of
the drunken class
Loud hailing from the Surrey towpath, ebb
tide to Barnes.

Kew

We ended our Thames Path walking tour
in Kew
Not in the ornamental flowering garden of
Eden
But tired and weary from our daily
journey
We slowly trekked across the trio of
granite arches
To descend onto the empty station
platform
Where we caught a Great Western back to
Waterloo
And then onto Winchester, our hometown

I had stared towards Strand on the Green
A Georgian parade of painted landscapes
Houses of actors, writers and Welsh poets
Dylan Thomas from the coal valleys of
South Wales
Drinking in the city atmosphere at the City
Barge
Where I had lost my innocence as a young
engineer
Another Celtic poet not blessed with
rhyme or reason.

I remember the West London traffic noise
And fashionable sixties' flying birds
Ferries moored at piled jetties and floating
pontoons
The aeroplanes overhead on their way to
Marseille
St Tropez in the South of France, Brigitte
Bardot!
Now a navigational aid for the Emirates
from Dubai
A third runway protest shout from an
island called Eel Pie.

Eel Pie Island

The Rolling Stones played to a teenage
dream
Now a ghost story with lost memories
Like the inventor, Trevor Bayliss
Who built a clever clockwork radio station
On a small Thames Island in the stream.

We walked together across the land-bridge
Back near half a twentieth century in my
mind
A boathouse looked out onto the old
towpath
Where royal barges rowed upriver to
Hampton Court
Ramshackle timber dwellings, the
dawning of Aquarius.

Ending Poem

The Thames towpath had fallen into canal-
side disrepair
With the onset of the Victorian Industrial
Revolution
And the coming of the London to
Southend Railway
East London became a smelly slum, a
graveyard shift
A dumping ground for sludge and slimy
effluent
At mucky Rainham Marshes and
Crossness spit
Building stone for Wren's great cathedral
arrived
On site from the spires of Oxford well
upstream
We walked from Joseph Conrad's Erith
westerly
Towards the gleaming new Thames Barrier
phenomenon
Via fresh perfumed lavender cologne and
oxygen
On our very Appendix Walk: a ten-mile
stretch
That ramblers said it was only for the hoi
pollio!

We were awestruck by the rocket space-
age behemoths
Marine engineering from a different planet
And on the Isle of Dogs? We never heard a
bark
Only a spark of genius, from the Royal
Academy
Before we reached old Greenland Dock
whaling station
Near Rotherhithe, where we kept out of
sight in Shad Thames
No Oliver Twist, Fagin or Bill Sykes, nor
Nancy's siren
Stage 1 on the Thames Path: Greenwich to
Tower Bridge
This time it was only a nine-mile easy stroll
on the flat
Stage 2: City Hall to Craven Cottage,
Putney on the opposite bank
A third day resurrection of the mind
within the Winchester diocese
Where I stood beside Wordsworth on
Westminster Bridge
Composing a sonnet for this parody song
of everlasting love.

Vauxhall Pleasure Gardens was where we
slept under the bright stars
Stage 3: Putney to Kew - to linger for a
while and reminisce
About nostalgia, not knowing about the
future pandemic
That nearly destroyed all our lives. But
some will survive.
Hammersmith Hospital was where Wendy
was born to a wartime bride
And a brave soldier who stayed behind
They lived close by before moving to
Strand on The Green
Where we had traipsed purposely along
the parapet and the gravel shore
Keats the cockney poet wrote a poem
about the bridge nearby
Having made a sole impression for us to
follow in his steps
We all remembered old friends without a
stoic smile or moan
Hilaire Belloc's prose built up the mighty
tidal Thames
That could be crossed on the ebb at Bronze
Kew.

We heard the swish of the tide on more
than twenty miles
From ebb to spring twice in a day, pulled
by the orange moon
Erith to Teddington, beyond Eel Pie where
we had walked before
Heart of Darkness was lit up without a
moan and with a smile!
Looking back, a year or two have passed
and Wendy and I never
Heard the ghostly wailing of Mary
Wollstonecraft
Who had tried to commit suicide by
leaping off Putney Bridge
Because her husband had run off with a
West End gaiety girl
But she was saved by an onlooker on
guard by the riverside
And so were we! To walk together for the
rest of our journey
Along the Thames Path to Teddington
Lock, the lower tidal limit
Reciting inspired poetry: *Adlestrop* and the
Lake Isle of Innisfree!